D1558638

GREAT SOCCER: Team Offense

Suzanne Cope

NEW HANOVER COUNTY
PUBLIC LIBRARY

HIGH
interest
books

Children's Press
A Division of Scholastic Inc.
New York / Toronto / London / Auckland / Sydney
Mexico City / New Delhi / Hong Kong
Danbury, Connecticut

Thanks to Carlos Giron and the girls' soccer team of St. Thomas Aquinas High School, Ft. Lauderdale, FL and Steve Lorenc and the boys' soccer team of Piper High School, Sunrise, FL.

Book Design: Christopher Logan
Contributing Editor: Matthew Pitt

Photo Credits: pp. 4, 8 © TempSport/Corbis; p.7 © Duomo/Corbis; Cover and all other photos by Maura Boruchow and Cindy Reiman

Visit Children's Press on the Internet at:
http://publishing.grolier.com

Library of Congress Cataloging-in-Publication Data

Cope, Suzanne.
    Great soccer : team offense / Suzanne Cope.
      p. cm. — (Sports clinic)
    Includes bibliographical references (p.) and index.
    ISBN 0-516-23167-7 (lib. bdg.) — ISBN 0-516-29563-2 (pbk.)
    1. Soccer—Offense—Juvenile literature. [I. Soccer.] I. Title. II. Series.

GV943.9.O44 C66 2001
796.334'2—dc21
                                                                    00-066050

Copyright 2001 by Rosen Book Works, Inc.
All rights reserved. Published simultaneously in Canada.
Printed in the United States of America.
1 2 3 4 5 6 7 8 9 10 R 05 04 03 02 01

CONTENTS

INTRODUCTION

Millions of women and men in Europe and South America consider it their favorite game. Here in the United States, we're finally learning how much fun it is. What game is this? Soccer! Soccer is one of the few team sports played all around the world. Americans are just beginning to catch on. You probably could find a league in your hometown.

Soccer teams have eleven players on each side. The object of the game is to score more goals than the other team. To do this, you have to put the ball into the other team's net. If you score the winning goal in a game, your team, your parents, and your fans will erupt with cheers. It's a thrilling feeling.

To score goals, you need to know how to shoot correctly. To do that, you have to know how to dribble. You must know how to "catch" the ball with your chest and pass it to teammates with your head. In other words, before you can score, you need to learn some basic skills. This book

Two players struggle for control of the ball.

introduces several drills that you can use to become a better player. You'll learn what the different positions on the team do. You'll also learn drills you can practice with one friend, a group of friends, or on your own. The more you practice, the sooner these drills will become skills. Once you learn the skills, you'll have a leg up on the other players!

This midfielder looks for a teammate to pass to.

MEET YOUR TEAM

Different Duties

Soccer teams have four different positions: forwards, midfielders, defenders, and goalkeepers. This chapter examines the different roles each position plays in a soccer game.

Forward

The main duty of a forward is to move the ball up the field and shoot at the other team's goal. Forwards sometimes also are called strikers. To be a great forward, you must have excellent dribbling and shooting skills. Some of the drills in Chapters 2 and 3 will help you along.

Midfielder

A midfielder's job is to help the forwards score goals by passing and dribbling. Midfielders, who also are called halfbacks, help the defense stop

Forwards spend hours of practice time trying to perfect their shooting skills.

the other team from scoring, too. They focus on the middle of the field and help the defense get the ball up to the forwards. Midfielders are usually excellent runners and can pass the ball well.

Defender

The duty of a defender is to keep the other team from scoring goals. Defenders, who also are known as fullbacks, must be aggressive. They also must be able to take the ball away from the other team's talented forwards.

FUN FACT:

People in countries such as Mexico, France, and Ireland call soccer by another name: football. Of course, it's very different from our version of football. They call the game football because, for the most part, players move the ball around the field with their feet.

A goalkeeper prepares to block a shot.

Goalkeeper

If a ball gets past the defense, it's up to the goalkeeper to stop it. Goalkeepers usually are called by their shortened name, goalies. Goalies are the only players who can touch the ball with their hands. They only can use their hands in the large goal box in front of the goal. The goal box area is marked with white, painted lines. Goalies must have strong leaping abilities. They also need

BASIC FORMATIONS

Forwards

Midfielders

Defenders

Goalie

Before each game, the coach must decide which formation to use.

good reflexes and quick hands to stop the ball from getting past them.

Formations

A soccer team usually has three forwards, three midfielders, four defenders, and one goalie. If the opposing team is very fast or has a great defense, a team might use a different formation, or mix of players. They might use four forwards or four mid-fielders. This combination gives the team more support in the middle of the field. The team can use their offensive skills more aggressively. The coach of each team decides which formation to use.

Pick Your Position

All of these positions work together as a team to try and win the game. Which position do you think would be right for you? If you think you'd be a good goalie, or a strong defender, check out the *Team Defense* book. If shooting sounds like music to your ears, read on!

FANCY FOOTWORK

Dribbling is when players use short, light kicks to move the ball around. One key to being a good dribbler is to keep the ball under control. Another key is to have the ability to dribble past opposing players.

While running across the field, the best dribblers kick the ball only a few feet in front of them. If you kick the ball too far ahead, the opposing team will have a better chance of taking it away. On the other hand, if you don't kick the ball far enough, your feet may get tripped up.

You can follow a few tips to improve your dribbling technique. Practice using both the inside and outside parts of your feet. Try not to kick with your toe. Don't stare at the ground or the ball. When possible, keep your head up, glancing at your opponents. Try to guess what their next moves will be before they make them.

The forward dribbles toward the goal, kicking the ball lightly.

Drills for Your Skills:

By Yourself:

Construct an obstacle course. Set up a series of plastic cones or empty water bottles. Place each one just a few feet apart from the next. Practice dribbling around the obstacles. Try to kick about three feet ahead with each dribble. It's harder than it looks!

Practice dribbling with both feet. You'll probably discover that one foot is easier to use than the other. The one that's easier to dribble with is your dominant, or stronger, foot. Great soccer players can dribble well with either foot.

With a Friend:

Have a friend play the full-back position while you

By setting up an obstacle course, offensive players can learn how to control the ball.

practice dribbling around him or her. Practice changing the direction of the ball using both the inside and outside of your foot. Start making up "fakeout" moves on your friend. When you make these moves, you pretend to dribble in one direction, but you actually move in another direction.

The best forwards can trick defenders into going in the wrong direction.

Another important skill in soccer offense is passing. Passing is when you kick the ball to teammates to get closer to the goal. The best passes reach players who are open, or unguarded, by other players. Passing should be done with the inside of your foot. Kick the ball in its center, using a strong, smooth motion. It's best to keep your "planted," or non-kicking, foot pointed in the direction that you want the ball to go.

If your teammate is standing still, kick the ball directly toward his or her feet. If your teammate is in motion, you must learn to lead him or her. Kick the ball a few steps ahead of where your teammate is on the field. In this way, he or she will be able to catch up to the ball without stopping. Soccer is a speedy game. The quicker and more accurate your passes are, the better chance you'll have at winning.

Strong and accurate passes often lead to goals.

Drills for Your Skills:

By Yourself:

Find a gym or playground wall that you're allowed to kick against, and practice passing to yourself. Pick a spot on the wall and kick to it. Work to get the rebound. Make sure your kicking motion is solid and straight, and try to keep the ball low to the ground.

With a Friend:

Practice the "give-and-go" strategy. Have a friend stand just ahead of you. Kick the ball to your friend and start running down the field, passing your friend by. Have him or her lead you with the ball by passing it ahead of where you're running. In a game, this strategy works best when the forward is moving down the sideline. Make sure you and your friend take turns giving and getting the pass.

These players have perfected the "give-and-go" strategy.

Pass back and forth with a friend. Practice this drill both while standing still and running up the field.

Practice crossing the ball. Crossing is when a teammate passes the ball from the corner or sideline to an open teammate standing in front of the goal. This type of pass is very important for offensive players to learn. A good crossing pass often leads to a goal!

Trapping is when you stop a ball flying directly toward you. Once you bring the ball under control, you can pass or shoot it toward the goal. To be good at trapping, you must not be afraid of the ball. Don't worry—it won't hurt! While the ball is in the air, make contact with the center of your forehead. Make sure your neck stays stiff and straight. Also, make sure you're looking at the ball just before you hit it so that you can aim where your header will go next.

When trapping with your head, be sure to keep your neck straight.

If the ball is not high enough to hit with your head, trap it with your chest. This kind of trapping takes some practice—so don't get discouraged. Keep your shoulders back and your breastbone aimed to catch the ball. The moment contact is made, relax your chest and let the ball drop softly to the ground.

You'll usually trap with your legs and feet. Don't try to stop the ball using just your foot. It could bounce right over you! When the ball makes contact with your legs or feet, "give" a bit. In other words, let your body relax and cradle the ball's impact. Remember when you were practicing passes against the gym wall? The wall was hard so the passes bounced right back to you. If you keep your body hard, the ball will bounce off of you, too. The problem is, it might bounce directly to your opponent! However, if you relax, the ball will drop right in front of you. Then you'll be in a perfect position to pass or shoot.

When trapping, players must give a little at the moment the ball first makes contact.

Drills for Your Skills

By Yourself:

Throw the ball in the air and practice trapping it with your head, chest, legs, and feet. As you get better, toss the ball higher. The higher you throw the ball, the more it can change directions on you in midair. This will prepare you for tough game situations.

Practice juggling. Try keeping the ball from touching the ground. Hit it softly into the air, using different parts of your body. Use your feet, ankles, chest, thighs, and head. With this kind of juggling, the only parts of your body you can't use are the hands!

With a Friend:

Throw the ball to a friend, having him or her trap it with different parts of the body. As the two of you get to be experts, have your friend approach you after the throw is made. Your friend will try to steal the ball, and you'll try to get around him or her. Don't forget to switch roles.

In a game, defenders will try to steal the ball from opposing midfielders and forwards.

SCORE!

GOING FOR THE GOAL

Getting goals is obviously how soccer games are won. Even though the goal is tall and wide, it's hard to score. Aiming with your feet is tough, and it takes practice to improve.

The basic form of shooting is similar to a hard pass. Keep your planted foot pointed toward the part of the goal that's your target. Swing the kicking leg solidly through the ball, striking it with your instep. The instep is the flat part on the top of your foot where your shoelaces begin. Try to kick the ball's bottom half without "scooping" it from underneath. Remember never to use your toe. You can injure yourself, and the kick won't be very accurate.

Great shooters aim for the open parts of the net. The goalie has no chance to stop this shot.

If you kick the ball right at the goalie every time you shoot, you'll probably be less effective. Try looking at open parts of the net as you make contact with the ball. The net's upper corners usually are good places to try.

It's always tricky deciding when to pass and when to shoot. Know your range, or how far away you can kick the ball into the net. If you're in range and there are no defenders blocking you, shoot! Remember to be a team player, though. If your teammate is open or has a better angle than you do, pass the ball.

Drills for Your Skills
By Yourself:
Go to a local field and practice shooting on goal from many different angles. Ask your coach if you can borrow a bag full of soccer balls. That way, you won't have to retrieve the ball every time you take a shot. Try to get into a shooting rhythm.

Set some soccer balls close to the net and others far away. Notice how close you need to be to have a strong, accurate shot. Work on improving your range.

This forward practices her shooting range.

With a Friend:

Practice your shot with a friend playing goalie. You also can use the open goal and practice shooting with a friend playing defense. Even the best shooters don't always shoot well under pressure. Learn to shoot well even when someone is challenging you for the ball.

Skilled offensive players learn to shoot from many different angles.

Throw-ins occur when the ball is kicked completely out of bounds on the sidelines. The team that didn't kick the ball out throws the ball in. The thrower stands behind the part of the sideline where the ball went out. During a throw-in, throwers must have both feet on the ground. They must throw the ball using both hands equally. The motion should come from behind the head and end in front. If the rules aren't followed, an illegal throw-in will be called and the opposing team will get the ball.

During throw-ins, offensive players should get open so the thrower has someone to throw to. It's a good strategy to move up and down the sideline. As with a pass, the thrower can throw to your feet. He or she also can lead you ahead of where you are so that you can run toward the ball.

Drills for Your Skills:

By Yourself:

Test your throw-in range. Practice and improve that range.

With a Friend:

Practice throw-ins with a friend. Have him or her trap the ball and throw it back.

Soccer players must perfect their throw-in technique, or they will risk losing the ball to their opponent.

Penalty Kicks:

When a serious offense, or foul, occurs within the goal box area, the referee calls for a penalty kick. Serious offenses include tripping and pushing opposing players or touching the ball with the hands. If the defending team is called for one of these fouls, the referee marks a line ten yards away from the net. Then the ref places the ball down and

gives a free kick to a forward on the opposing team. This means that the goalie is the only player who can defend the shot. All other players must stand outside the goal box until the forward kicks the ball. Penalty kicks often decide a game, so forwards definitely should practice for this situation.

Make certain you shoot a penalty kick using a strong, fluid motion.

GAME PLAN

Now that you've practiced your drills and picked up some skills, it's time to put them to good use. This chapter suggests several ways you can use your new skills on the soccer field. You'll see how these skills can help you score goals and win games!

Once you've mastered dribbling, try some fake-out moves. These also are called changes-of-direction. You move your body one way but then kick in the other. Use your imagination when trying to fake-out the other team. Only you will know the exact direction of the ball. You'll leave the defender in the dust! Practice moving the ball with both your left and right foot and with the outside and inside of each foot.

Forwards must be able to control the ball with both feet.

It's important to dribble at the right times. Dribble when there are only one or two opponents between you and the goal. Try running down the sidelines. Since opponents only can be on one side of you, you'll have more room to move.

You should know when to pass as well as dribble. If your teammate is open, or standing, or running in front of the goal, pass him or her the ball. Remember that no one wins a soccer game alone.

Passing Game

As an offensive player, you're trying to move the ball toward the goal with the help of teammates. The best way to do this is with a combination of dribbling and passing. Pass a teammate the ball when he or she is closer to the goal than you are or when no defenders are nearby. After you make your pass, move around and try to slip by your defender. Once you get open, you'll get the ball passed back to you. Try the give-and-go or lead your teammate to an open spot on the field. Don't be afraid to talk to your teammates. Tell them when a defender is near or when you're open.

In the Net

Now that you're near the net, let's take the next step—scoring goals. When you get within your range, try for a shot. Because of pressure from defending fullbacks, shots on goal often must be made quickly. Therefore, you should practice "one-touching" the ball. This means timing your kick so that you shoot the instant you receive your teammate's pass. Since you won't always have time to set up for a shot, practice shooting off-balance. Remember not to focus on the goalie. Try to aim for a corner or the area of the net farthest from the goalie.

Don't forget that a goal doesn't have to be scored with your foot. When the ball is in flight, try and head it or bounce it off your thigh or knee. The juggling and trapping skills you practiced will come in handy here. A goal doesn't have to be pretty—it only needs to make it into the net!

Using Your Head

If you like soccer, the most important thing to do is play. Get involved! If you're interested in joining a soccer team, try your local youth council or community center. Often each town will have summer, fall, and even spring leagues. Join your school's team. Try getting tickets to a game played by a professional or semiprofessional league.

In the sport of soccer, you use individual skills to help your team win. By developing your skills over time and working hard during practice, you'll help your team both on and off the field. When you're at practice, focus on doing the skills correctly each time. Recognize which of your skills need work. Then spend time improving those areas. You will help your team by becoming a better player. You also will feel better about yourself because you've strengthened your soccer skills.

It's important to have a good attitude as well as good skills. Remember that no one gets better at soccer without a lot of practice. Even forwards

Whether you win or lose, always congratulate the other side for their strong effort.

and midfielders who play professionally started where you're starting now. Keep a positive attitude during games. Play within the rules. Remember that it is only a game, and both teams should have fun. No matter who wins, congratulate your teammates and the other team on a game well played. Continue to improve your skills and show good sportsmanship. That way you'll be a champion, no matter what the final score is.

change-of-direction a strategy where a player pretends to go one way and then kicks in another way

defenders players who try to stop the other team from scoring

dominant stronger

dribbling kicking the ball just ahead of your feet

formation the combination of different positions on the field

forwards players whose main job it is to shoot and score on the opposing team's goal

goalkeepers players responsible for guarding the net from the opposing team's shots

leading passing or throwing the ball ahead of a teammate

midfielders players who set up goals by passing the ball to the forwards

opponents soccer players on another team

range the farthest distance that a player is able to kick or throw the ball well

shooting kicking the ball toward the goal in an attempt to score

trapping stopping the ball with your body

FOR FURTHER READING

Anderson, Dave. *The Story of the Olympics.* New York: HarperCollins Publishers, 2000.

Christopher, Matt. *On the Field With Mia Hamm.* Boston: Little, Brown, and Company, 1998.

Weber, Chloe. *Mia Hamm Rocks!* New York: Welcome Rain Publishing, 1999.

Woods, Paula. *Improve Your Soccer Skills.* London: Usborne House, 1993.

Woog, Dan. *20 Steps to Better Soccer.* Chicago: Lowell House, 2000.

RESOURCES

Organizations

Alliance of Youth Sports Organizations
P. O. Box 351
South Plainfield, NJ 07080
E-mail: info@aoyso.com

American Youth Soccer Organization (AYSO)
12501 South Isis Avenue
Hawthorne, CA 90250

RESOURCES

Web Sites

Soccer America

http://www.socceramerica.com/

The home page of Soccer America magazine, this Web site features a youth link along with information about soccer camps and the U.S. National team.

Internet Soccer

http://internetsoccer.com/

This Web site gives you links to soccer news from around the world. There's also a link that shows you what other youth soccer teams are doing.

INDEX

GREAT SOCCER: TEAM OFFENSE

About the Author

Suzanne Cope is a freelance writer and avid soccer player who lives in Boston, Massachusetts. She has been playing soccer since she was 12 years old. Suzanne also coaches youth soccer and referees in her spare time. Her favorite position to play is fullback.

ML   11/01